BACKBONE DRUMS
An introduction to playing and understanding the drum kit
By Dave Hazlewood

Foundation level
Edited by Rob Woodcock

PUBLISHING

Knowle farm business centre, Wadhurst road,
Frant, East Sussex, TN3 9EJ
United Kingdom
www.one8e.co.uk

ISBN 978-0-9567790-0-7

Backbone drums – Foundation level
This volume: 1st edition
© Copyright 2010 Dave Hazlewood

Dave Hazlewood has asserted his right
to be identified as the author of this work
in accordance with the Copyright,
Designs and Patents Act 1988

Produced by one8e publishing
Published by one8e publishing
All rights reserved

Printed in England by CPI UK

Edited by Rob Woodcock
Cover design by Andy McIntosh

Dedications

In writing these books I have realised how lucky I am to be doing what I love for a living and how many good people there are around me helping me along. I would like to say a big thank you to everyone that has helped and supported me along the way...

To my wife Sam and my parents Dave and Julie for believing in me and listening to me rant when things don't go right.

My friends for life, Ben Wilks, Phil Mason, Andy Sloman, Rob Woodcock, Paul Cheese and Dan Wright for being there whenever I need them.

My fellow teachers, Mike Brazier, Mike Small, David Driver and Richard Davey for being part of our network and for giving me feedback on these books.

Andy McIntosh, Matt Norton, Dan Wright and Paul Cheese for going beyond the call of duty helping me get this project off the ground.

Colin Woolway for inspiring me and taking me seriously over the years.

Carl at Animal Custom Drums and Martin at Korg (Paiste Cymbals/Vic Firth drum sticks) for keeping me supplied with top notch drums and cymbals.

All my students that have stuck with me over the years.

The Anti-Nowhere League and 4th Wall for keeping me playing and doing what I do...

Contact details

For more information about one8e publishing or one8e studio please contact Dave Hazlewood.
Tel: +44 (0) 1892 750157
Email: info@one8e.co.uk
Web: www.one8e.co.uk

For more information on Backbone Drums please contact Dave Hazlewood
Tel: +44 (0) 1892 750157
Email: info@one8e.co.uk
www.backbonedrums.com

Backbone Drums

Introduction

Welcome to the first Backbone drums book. This is the foundation level book and covers all of the basic elements of playing drums. At the end of this book, you will know what your role as a drummer is within a band, be able to play a variety of simple beats and fills, create your own ideas and most importantly understand how the drum kit works as a musical instrument.

As the series of books progress, you will learn new styles, techniques and concepts aimed at developing your drumming and expanding your knowledge.

Drums are the backbone of any band and the drummer has a vital part to play in making a successful band. This series of books is designed to be the backbone of a drummer's knowledge by looking into a huge number of concepts, techniques and styles. I do not claim to cover every element in complete depth, but instead give an understanding and awareness of what is important for any drummer to know.

This is your 'Backbone' of knowledge!

From here you can choose to specialise or work more in depth on the things that you find most relevant and interesting.

With many years of professional drumming experience gigging, touring, recording and teaching, these books have been written and arranged in a practical order, with an aim of giving the most realistic lesson structure to a student wanting to apply their drumming in the real world. This is not just about passing exams!!!

Teachers using this material will not only be using these books and backing tracks, but will also have access to online progress records and extra material to make your learning even more organised and successful.

Good luck, take your time and have fun!!!

Drum Lesson Manager

Teachers subscribing to the 'Backbone Drums Lesson Manager' will have access to more material, lesson plans and online progress records to help deliver the best lessons possible and motivate students. Students studying with these teachers will benefit from structured lessons, clear goals for practice, and will be able to view their progress record, practice targets and awards online.

For information on
Backbone Drums Lesson Manager visit:
www.backbonedrums.com

Contents

Backing track list

Backing tracks - Suitable for exercises from chapters one - five
1. 60bpm Pop ballad
2. 65bpm Rock ballad
3. 65bpm Goth rock
4. 75bpm Pop rock
5. 75bpm Heavy rock
6. 85bpm Groove pop
7. 90bpm Classic rock
8. 95bpm Dark pop
9. 110bpm Bubblegum pop
10. 160bpm Alternative rock

Backing tracks - Suitable for exercises from chapter six
11. 60bpm Modern blues
12. 70bpm Classic blues
13. 85bpm Blues rock

Chart tracks - To accompany the charts from chapter seven
14. Chart 2 with drums
15. Chart 2 with click
16. Chart 3 with drums
17. Chart 3 with click
18. Chart 5 with drums
19. Chart 5 with click
20. Chart 7 with drums
21. Chart 7 with click

Click tracks – Suitable for exercises from any chapter
22. Click @ 60bpm
23. Click @ 65bpm
24. Click @ 70bpm
25. Click @ 75bpm
26. Click @ 80bpm
27. Click @ 85bpm
28. Click @ 90bpm
29. Click @ 95bpm
30. Click @ 100bpm
31. Click @ 105bpm
32. Click @ 110bpm
33. Click @ 115bpm
34. Click @ 120bpm

BPM – Beats Per Minute
Speed in music is called 'Tempo' and is measured in 'beats per minute'. All backing tracks contain a click which marks this time and occur on every quarter note.

Throughout this book you will see 'bpm' written a lot to either give you an idea of how fast you are playing or to give you goals to work towards.

Backing track guide

The first part of the CD-ROM contains backing tracks for you to play exercises from this book along with. There are several ways to use the backing tracks provided, which will become more apparent the further you get through the book.

Groove playing

Initially looping one exercise along with a track will help to develop your timing and will be a great way to gauge your progress. When you feel you are ready to be more adventurous, refer back to this page to see how else you can use the backing tracks.

Four bar phrasing

Each section in all of the backing tracks is written in groups of four bars, so you are able to loop four bar phrases all the way through a track and feel where the sections change without getting out of sync with the song.

Song structures

Backing tracks 1 - 10 and 13 have the same structure.

A – Four bars – Intro/bridge (or extended chorus)

B – Four bars – Verse (part A)

B – Four bars – Verse (part B)

C – Four bars – Chorus

This arrangement is repeated four times

Backing tracks 11 and 12 are in a twelve bar blues format. This is where a piece of music follows a particular chord progression over twelve bars that gives it a very specific sound and is just like a twelve bar phrase.

Listen to the backing tracks to hear how the music changes from section to section, and then see how you can play each song more musically by playing a different groove for each section and fills that help move between them.

Chart writing

This is your chance to be really creative writing drum parts and will be a great exercise to prepare you for playing with a real band. If by the end of this book if you are totally happy with reading music, you could have a go at writing your ideas down in the form of a chart! Remember the arrangement (ABBC) is repeated four times and each time through doesn't have to be the same, feel free to experiment by maybe making the third time through completely different from the others.

Only attempt this if you are completely happy with everything in this book and you are working with a drum teacher as this will be difficult to complete on your own with no guidance!

Reading and rudiment practice

Although the click tracks (22 – 34) are ideal for practicing reading exercises or rudiments, it is a good idea to play your rudiments along with the musical backing tracks (with click) as well. Playing a Paradiddle or double stroke roll along with a rock track at 85bpm will be more interesting than playing to just a click at 85bpm, and will help you to develop a more musical feel.

Book guide

In writing these books, I have not given the note values their classical names, but instead have used a more modern approach and used names based around fractions. This approach is a lot more common now and in a lot of places has become the standard way to refer to note values. Teaching this makes the whole process a lot more logical and easy to understand and learn.

To clarify, here is a list of the modern note names used in these books with their classical names next to them:

Whole note ----------------------- Semi-breve

Half note ------------------------ Minim

Quarter note -------------------- Crotchet

Eighth note ---------------------- Quaver

Sixteenth note ------------------- Semi-quaver

Although you don't need to know the classical names to work through this book and understand note values, they are still used in certain situations, so you need to know them. Refer back to this page when you have completed the book.

Note positions

The key used in this book for which drum is on which line of the stave, is the most commonly used key, but you may come across variations in some tuition books. There has never been a universal standard key used worldwide, but the key I have used has been the standard for most drummers and authors for some time now.

Left handed drummers

Any exercise in this book that require either a left or right hand to play a specific note has been written from a right-handed players point of view. Left-handed players should reverse any instructions that state left and right.

Signing off and moving on

At the bottom of most pages within this book and the rest of the series you will see a box titled 'Signing off and moving on'. This has targets that you should aim to achieve before moving on to the next page or section. These targets are broken down into bronze, silver and gold with bronze being the minimum requirement, silver being acceptable and gold being a good standard at which to progress.

Although it is preferable to sign off at gold standard before moving on, it is not essential and if you are struggling with any section you should just make a note of what level you have achieved and move on. You can always go back and re-do any weaker sections at a later date.

In the beginning

Quarter Note

In chapter one you will learn the absolute basics of playing drums.

Checklist

By the end of this chapter you should be able to achieve the following:

- **Name all parts of the drum kit**
- **Explain the role of a drummer in a band**
- **Name all drum and cymbal positions on a stave**
- **Explain what a repeat sign and a repeat last bar sign mean**
- **Explain what a groove is**
- **Explain what a fill is**
- **Play quarter note grooves**
- **Play quarter note fills**
- **Play four bar phrases**
- **Play along with backing tracks**
- **Create your own fills and play in four bar phrases**

Use this page as an end of chapter test. When you have completed chapter one, come back to this page and see if you can complete the list above.

For information on
Backbone Drums Lesson Manager visit:
www.backbonedrums.com

Kit recognition

A drum kit is made up of 'drums' and 'cymbals'.

The picture above is of a standard 5-piece drum kit. '5-piece' refers to the number of drums only and does not include cymbals or stands.

In a standard 5 piece drum kit there is a bass drum, a snare drum and three tom toms (normally just called 'toms' and are sometimes referred to as 1st, 2nd and floor toms).

The cymbals shown here include a pair of hi-hats, a ride cymbal and two crash cymbals.

The other bits (not labelled) that make up the drum kit are the hi-hat stand and two cymbal stands. There will also be a drum stool to sit on.

- **Please note that the hi-hat pedal is not used at this level, but will be introduced in the level one book.**

Signing off and moving on
• *Correctly identify each drum and cymbal on your own drum kit or teachers drum kit* •
Gold - All correct

Drum kit basic notation

To play and understand the exercises in this book, you will need to understand from the beginning a bit about how music written and presented. This will help your learning, but will also ensure that as a drummer you have all of the knowledge and understanding to be a great musician.

Here are the most basic elements of reading music that you will see. You will learn more as you progress.

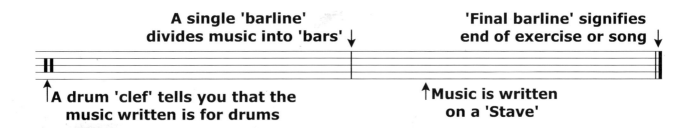

A single 'barline' divides music into 'bars' ↓   **'Final barline' signifies end of exercise or song** ↓

↑**A drum 'clef' tells you that the music written is for drums**   ↑**Music is written on a 'Stave'**

Where a note is situated on the stave tells us which drum or cymbal to hit. As a rough guide, 'the higher up the stave, the higher up the drum kit.' This is only a general rule and will depend slightly on how you set up your drums.

A cross written on the stave lets you know that you need to hit something metal (i.e. cymbals).

Crash   **Hi-hats**   **Ride**   **Stepped hi-hats**

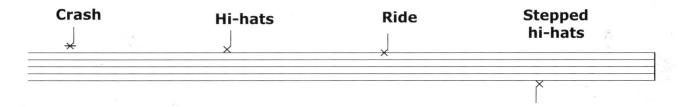

A dot on the stave lets you know to play a drum.

1st tom   **2nd tom**   **Snare drum**   **Floor tom**   **Bass drum**

A drum kit is made up of two instruments, drums and cymbals. When drum kit music is written, it is quite often written as two parts. This is shown in this example where the cymbal pattern is written above the drum pattern

Signing off and moving on
• *Correctly identify which drum and cymbal goes on which line of the stave* •
Gold - All correct

Quarter note groove

Music on any instrument is broken up into bars just as speech is broken up into words. Below is one bar of drum music where you will play the hi-hats, bass drum and snare drum. Your lead (stronger) hand plays four hi-hats, while your lead (stronger) foot and opposite hand alternate playing the bass drum and snare drum.

The first and third hi-hats are played in time with the bass drum, while the second and fourth hi-hats are played in time with the snare.

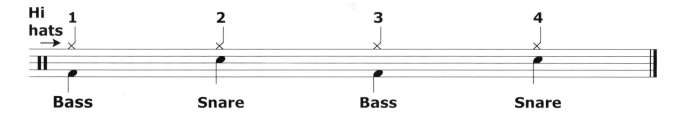

What you have just played is a basic 'groove' (also known as a 'beat' or 'rhythm'). A drummer's primary job is to keep time for a band and this is usually done by playing a groove over and over again. The most common grooves in modern music are based on an alternating bass drum and snare drum. Listen to some of your favourite songs and listen out for that sound (bass - snare - bass - snare).

When you are comfortable with this first groove, start to loop (repeat) it and play it along with a backing track.

Quarter note fill

Different sections of a song may have different types of grooves, so to help flow from one section to another drummers also play fills.

Below is a basic fill using the snare drum, first, second and floor toms.
Play each beat with your lead hand.

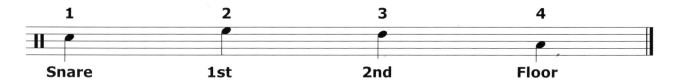

Try playing the groove and then the fill at the same speed without speeding up or slowing down. When you are comfortable alternate between the groove and fill.

<hr>

Signing off and moving on
• *Loop just the groove consistently with a rock or pop backing track* •
Gold - 160bpm
Silver - 90bpm
Bronze - 65bpm

Quarter note four bar phrase

Fills are played far less often than grooves and you may play long sections with no fills at all. Because of this you need to know when you do play a fill that it is in the correct place.

Most modern music is written in sections, which are quite often in groups of four bars, so practicing playing fills in every fourth bar, will get you used to how that feels and make it easier to incorporate fills into our playing.

This is known as a four bar phrase (three bars of groove and one bar of fill) and is written out below. Note that the first bar of groove now starts with a crash instead of a hi-hat. This works well when coming out of the fill and going back into the groove when repeating.

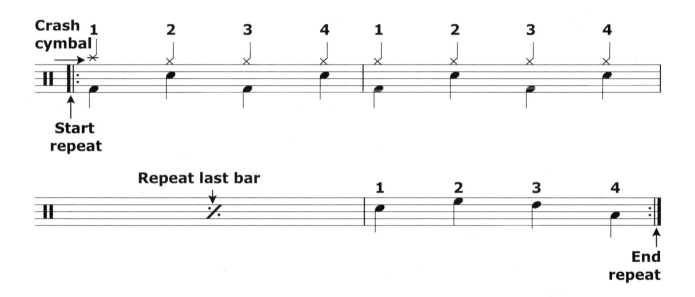

Crash cymbal - Play a crash cymbal instead of a hi-hat at the start of each four bar phrase

Repeat last bar - When the same drum groove is played several times in a row, this sign is used instead of writing out the groove in every bar. Just play the same as the last bar.

Start repeat/End repeat - When you see these bar lines, you are required to play everything between them for a second time. When you get to the 'end repeat' sign, go back to the 'start repeat' sign and play through again. If there is an 'end repeat' sign, but no 'Start repeat' sign, you go back to the start of the piece.

When you are comfortable with this exercise play every other four bar phrase on the ride cymbal instead of the hi-hats.

Signing off and moving on
• *Play the four bar phrase looped with a rock or pop backing track* •
Gold - 160bpm
Silver - 90bpm
Bronze - 65bpm

More fill ideas

Now that you have mastered playing the quarter note groove and fill in four bar phrases, let's be a bit more creative.

Below are five exercises that can be played as fills within your four bar phrases. Start slowly and play four bar phrases with a backing track when you feel comfortable.

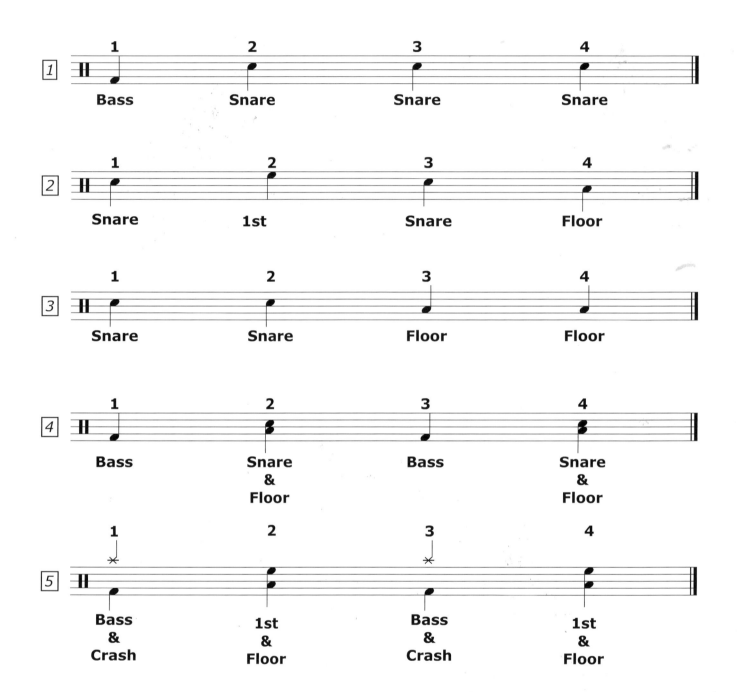

Copyright © D. Hazlewood

Create your own fills using quarter notes

Now it's your turn!!! Use the blank manuscript below to make your own fills. Be as creative as you want, but make sure you keep your fills in time. Try to write the notes on the correct lines, but don't write the drum names as this will help you learn where each drum and cymbal sits on the stave.

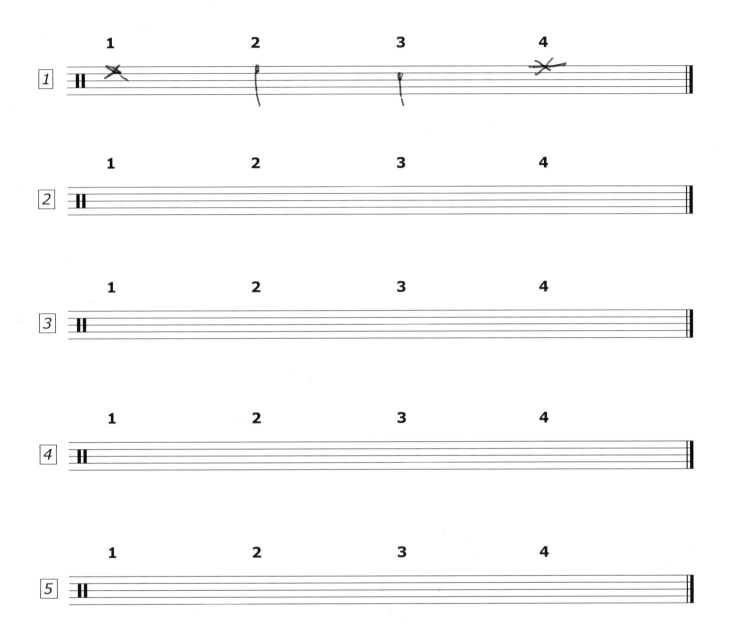

Then there were eight

Eighth Note **Two Eighth Notes** **Four Eighth Notes**

In chapter two, we look at playing eighth notes in grooves and fills and start to get a bit more creative with the bass drum. A single eighth note looks different from a quarter note in that it has a 'tail'. When you get two or four eighth notes together they join their tails (see above).

Checklist

By the end of this chapter you should be able to achieve the following:

- **Play eighth note grooves**

- **Play eighth note fills**

- **Read music containing quarter notes and eighth notes**

- **Play fills mixing quarter notes and eighth notes**

- **Create your own fills mixing quarter notes and eighth notes**

- **Play quarter notes and eighth notes as snare and bass drum patterns**

- **Play quarter note and eighth note snare and bass patterns with eighth note hi-hats**

- **Play quarter note and eighth note snare and bass patterns with quarter note hi-hats**

- **Create your own grooves using quarter notes and eighth notes as snare and bass patterns**

- **Understand what a time signature is and what 4/4 means**

As in chapter one, use this page as an end of chapter test. When you have completed chapter two, come back to this page and see if you can complete the list above.

For information on
Backbone Drums Lesson Manager visit:
www.backbonedrums.com

Eighth note groove

This next groove is similar to the first in that the snare and bass pattern is exactly the same, but the hi-hat pattern has changed. Your lead (stronger) hand is now playing twice as many hi-hats, which means there is an extra hit in between each count. To help count and play this we will say 'and' (written as '+') in between our count. Because you are playing more notes, you may need to play this groove a bit slower to start.

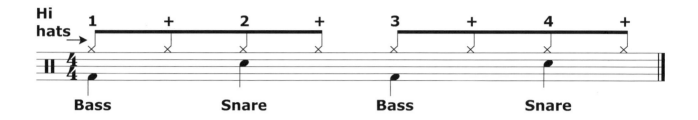

When you are comfortable with this groove, play it along with a backing track. Experiment playing the groove on the ride instead of the hi-hats.

Eighth note fill

As well as using eighth notes in grooves, we can play them in fills. Below is a basic fill using eighth notes. When you feel comfortable, alternate between the groove and fill maintaining a steady tempo.

Signing off and moving on
• *Play the four bar phrase looped with a rock or pop backing track* •
Gold - 110bpm
Silver - 85bpm
Bronze - 60bpm

Copyright © D. Hazlewood

Eighth note four bar phrase

Just as we did with the quarter note groove and fill, we are going to play the eighth note groove and fill in four bar phrases.

Notice the new sign at the start of the piece!

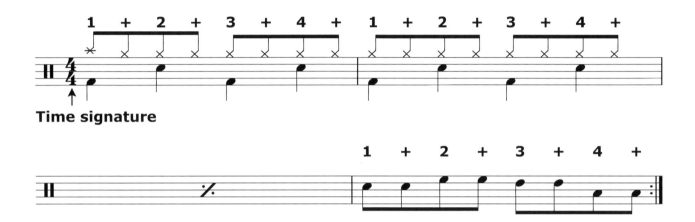

Time signature

When you are comfortable with this exercise have a go at playing every other four bar phrase on the ride cymbal instead of the hi-hats, then play along with a backing track

Time signature - A time signature is something you will always see at the start of a piece of music. It tells you how many beats are in a bar and what each beat is worth.

The top number tells you how many beats are in a bar (this is what you count and gives a piece of music its 'pulse' or 'feel'), in this case four.

The bottom number tells you what type of note it is that you are counting, in this case the bottom '4' represents quarters.

4/4 is the most common time signature used and is sometimes simply written as 'C'.

There are several different time signatures and they can be read as if they were fractions:
ie. 4/4 = four quarter notes per bar. 3/4 = three quarter notes per bar. 6/8 = six eighth notes per bar.

Don't worry if this is a bit confusing, 4/4 will be the only time signature we shall be using for now and we shall only go further into time signatures much later when we need to.

Signing off and moving on
• Play the four bar phrase looped with a rock or pop backing track •
Gold - 110bpm
Silver - 85bpm
Bronze - 60bpm

Mixing quarter notes and eighth notes

We have looked at quarter notes and eighth notes on their own, but it is possible to mix them up within one bar. By mixing different notes within one bar, you can create some interesting rhythms.

Reading exercises for the snare drum

With all reading exercises like this make sure you follow these few simple rules to aid learning and develop timing.

- **Make sure you have a strong count and count out loud.**

- **Keep the numbers nice and even**
  (in this exercise ensure that the '+' count is placed exactly between the numbers).

- **Play with a click track.**

- **Tap your foot in time with the click track to help with timing.**

Play the following snare exercises one at a time and then play the whole page as one exercise:

Copyright © D. Hazlewood

Quarter notes and eighth notes around the drums as fills

Now you are comfortable with the timing of playing quarter notes and eighth notes together, we can take the same rhythms and play them around the drums as fills.

Play the following fills slowly on their own to make sure you are playing the correct rhythms, and then using either the quarter note or the eighth note groove play them as fills in four bar phrases.

STICKING - When we refer to 'sticking' we are talking about which hand plays which note. All stickings have been written for right-handed players, so apologies to left-handed drummers, but you will have to reverse all stickings.

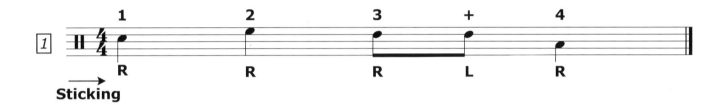

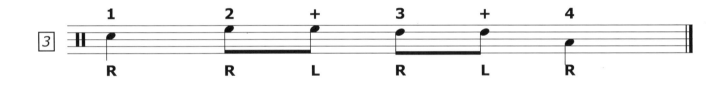

Signing off and moving on
• Play each of these fills with any groove in four bar phrases with a rock or pop backing track •
Gold - 110bpm
Silver - 85bpm
Bronze - 60bpm

Create your own fills using quarter notes and eighth notes

Use the blank manuscript below to make your own fills. Be as creative as you like, but make sure you keep your fills in time. Write the notes on the correct lines, but don't write the drum names in as this will help you learn where each drum and cymbal sits on the stave.

When you feel confident enough, play each of your fills in four bar phrases with either the quarter note or eighth note groove along with backing tracks

Copyright © D. Hazlewood

Quarter notes and eighth notes as snare drum and bass drum patterns

You are now used to mixing quarter notes and eighth notes in fills, so you have lots of fills but so far only two grooves!!! Time to change that...

If you take the quarter note and eighth note patterns from page 12 which we made into fills on page 13, split them between your bass drum and snare drum and add either of the hi-hat patterns you can create lots of interesting grooves.

Here are the same four patterns from page 12 but split between the bass drum and snare drum.

- **Only the notes that fall on counts 2 and 4 are played on the snare drum.**

- **All other notes played on the bass drum**

Play the following four exercises with no hi-hats. Don't play the snare drum with your lead hand as this will need to be free to play hi hats when we add them.

Eighth note grooves
with varied bass patterns

The next four grooves combine the previous snare drum and bass drum exercises with an eighth note hi-hat pattern. The grooves will sound similar to the first eighth note groove you played from page 10, but has extra bass drums, which will make the groove more interesting and musical.

A common way to make drum grooves work within music is to follow the rhythms played by other instruments with the bass drum. Listen to some rock or pop tunes to hear how the drum pattern works with the other instruments.

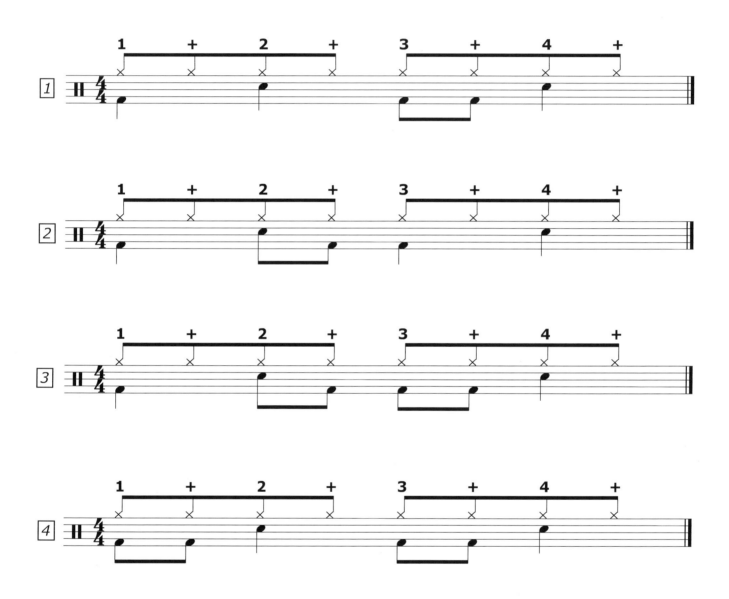

Quarter notes grooves
with varied bass patterns

The next four grooves combine the snare drum and bass drum exercises with quarter note hi-hats which sound effective, but may initially be a bit tricker to play as some of the bass drums are played on their own in-between the hi-hats. This element of drumming is referred to as 'independence'.

Independence

Independent means not dependent or influenced by anything else. An independent limb is therefore not dependent on or influence by any other limb. This means that through study and practice we can have four limbs independent of each other and able to play four completely different things. When you first play these grooves you may find you automatically play a hi-hat with the bass drums on the '+' count, but as your independence improves you will find your hi-hat hand will play consistent quarter notes whatever bass drum pattern you play.

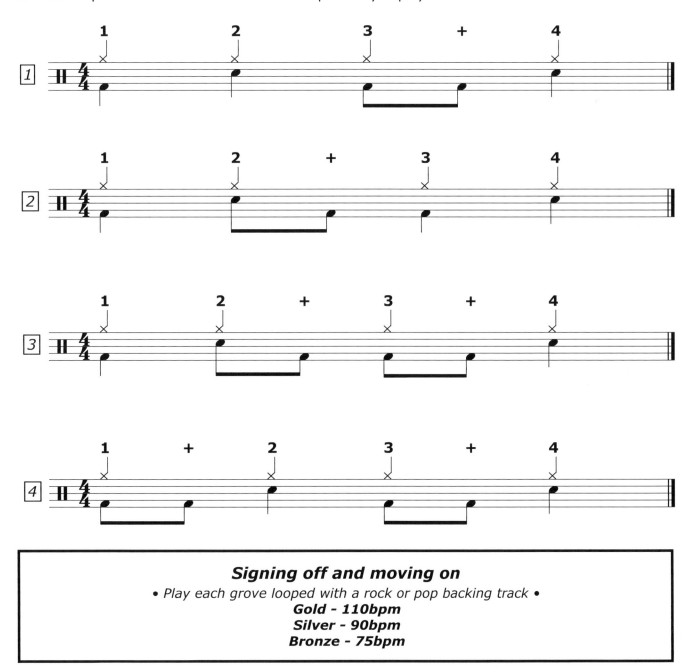

```
┌──────────────────────────────────────────────────────────────┐
│              Signing off and moving on                        │
│   • Play each grove looped with a rock or pop backing track • │
│                   Gold - 110bpm                               │
│                   Silver - 90bpm                              │
│                   Bronze - 75bpm                              │
└──────────────────────────────────────────────────────────────┘
```

Create your own grooves

Now have a go at making some grooves of your own. Write some snare and bass patterns into the four exercises below, or you can use the rhythms you made up for fills on page 14, or make some new rhythms, and split them between your snare drum and bass drum.

Remember...

- **Only the notes that fall on counts 2 and 4 are played on the snare drum.**

- **All other notes are played on the bass drum.**

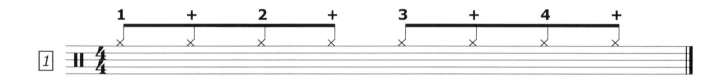

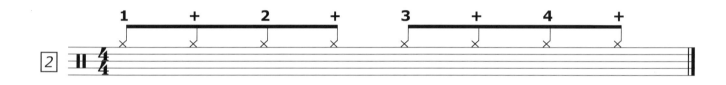

Signing off and moving on
• *Play each grove looped with a rock or pop backing track* •
Gold - 110bpm
Silver - 85bpm
Bronze - 60bpm

That's the way to do it

In the first two chapters we have learnt to play different grooves and fills, but with any musical instrument how we play something is just as important as what we play.

It is very important to remember that it is better to play something simple but well executed, rather than something complicated poorly executed.

Checklist

By the end of this chapter, you should be able to achieve the following:

- **Explain the importance of good technique within your playing**

- **Demonstrate good posture**

- **Demonstrate good grip**

- **Demonstrate good bass drum technique**

- **Explain what rudiments are and why we practice them**

- **Play nice and even single stroke rolls with a click track**

- **Play nice and even double stroke rolls with a click track**

- **Play nice and even paradiddles with a click track**

- **Apply rudiments to fills**

As in previous chapters, use this page as an end of chapter test. When you have completed chapter three, come back to this page and see if you can complete the list above.

For information on
Backbone Drums Lesson Manager visit:
www.backbonedrums.com

What is technique?

Technique is the way we do something. So far we have looked at what to play, but now it's time to look at how we play.

Good technique can make the following improvements to our playing:

- **Better sound from the drums and cymbals**

- **More even placement of notes**

- **Louder when needed**

- **Quieter when needed**

- **Faster when needed**

- **Slower when needed**

- **Improved timing**

- **Improved musicality**

- **Good technique will also help to avoid injury and will require less energy and exertion.**

Good technique checklist:

Relax – Tension is your enemy!
If there is tension anywhere in your body, it will spread and work against you. Make sure you are totally relaxed when playing and everything will sound better and happen much easier.

Good posture – Sit up straight and pull your shoulders back – DO NOT slouch or lean over your drum kit. Avoid looking at the ground when you play, but instead keep your head up.

Good grip - Anyone can pick up a bit of wood and hit a drum, but it takes a bit more work to do it well. Initially, you may find that your grip doesn't affect your playing, so why practice to improve it? As you progress and want to play more complicated and exciting drum parts, you will need complete control over your drum sticks and this can only be achieved with good grip. You might as well start getting it right now!

Which grip for me?

With many techniques that we use as drummers, there are quite often variations and options available to us. Some techniques help us to express ourselves in a certain way, whereas others are just personal preference. Watch a few top drummers playing and you will notice that they don't all play in exactly the same way, but instead all have individual styles.

There are several main variations of grip, there is no reason why you shouldn't learn and use all variations, but I recommend that initially you start with 'German matched grip' as I believe this to be the most versatile.

Here are the three main variations:

Traditional grip – This is the most traditional grip and goes back to the early days of military marching bands. Each hand holds the stick differently. The lead hand holds the stick from the top and the other hand holds the stick from underneath. This originally helped a marching drummer play over the side of his drum that would be carried at an angle. Traditional grip is still used today by lots of drummers and is especially popular with jazz drummers.

Matched grip (French) – The most common modern grip is the matched grip where both hands hold the stick in the same way. This aids movement around a modern drum kit and can be more efficient.

With French matched grip the palms of the hands face into each other and the fingers are used a lot to help move the stick. This is a common grip, but some say that it lacks power due to the use of fingers more than wrist.

Matched grip (German) – As in French matched grip, both hands hold the stick the same way in German matched grip but is different from the French grip in that the palms of the hands face down to the floor rather than into each other. This then relies more on wrist action to move the stick and can achieve a lot of power

Foot technique

We have looked at upper body technique, so we also need to look at technique for our feet. Many people spend a massive amount of time developing their hand technique, but tend to overlook their feet, which can lead to a playing imbalance.

Which foot technique for me?

As with grip, there are various options available to us for our foot technique. Again, some choices are down to personal preference, but there are different techniques for different jobs. For example, one technique will help you play faster, whereas a different technique may help you to play quieter.

Initially, I would suggest comfort as a deciding factor to getting your foot technique working for you. We will re-visit this subject in future books.

Heel down – This is a very relaxed technique, as your foot is left resting on the pedal with all of the work being done by your ankle. This is a good technique that gives a good open sound from the bass drum and gives a lot of control when using the hi-hat pedal. You may however find playing very fast or very loud a bit trickier with this technique.

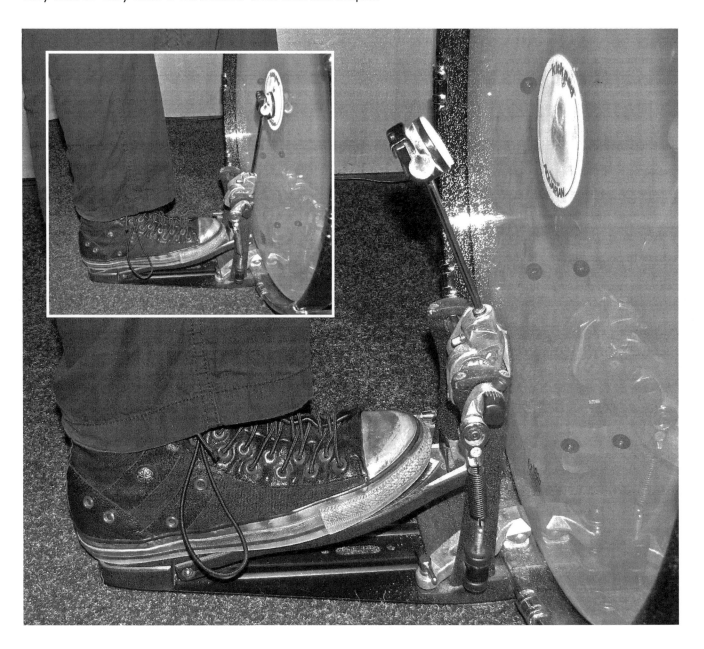

Heel up – This is a very powerful technique as the weight of your leg gets behind each stroke. This is a better technique for playing louder, but is not so relaxed as you have to lift your leg to play each stroke and then holds your foot in place when not playing. You can also get a much deader sound from a bass drum because the bass drum beater tends to stay pushed (or 'buried') into the drum head. With this technique, you will have less control and may find it difficult to play softer.

With all hand and foot techniques, you should use what works for you. Some techniques will take longer to master, so don't be too quick to dismiss them.

Remember to stay relaxed and make sure that whatever techniques you use, you don't put any stress on your joints and if something hurts, stop and review what you are doing straight away.

What are rudiments?

Rudiments are basic exercises that all drummers need to practice to improve technique and general playing. Normally, we start by playing these on just one drum or on a practice pad (rubber pad for quieter practice) to focus on the details of how we play, so that when we return to the drum kit we naturally play better.

Traditional rudiments are intended to be played with the hands, but a more modern approach is to apply rudiments to our feet as well. Initially, we shall be taking the traditional route of playing rudiments with our hands, but feel free to experiment and try the same exercises with your feet (especially if you like the idea of playing fast bass drum patterns on the drum kit).

Practice all rudiments with a click track.

Single stroke roll

This is the first and most important rudiment to get right. Although you will use this as an exercise to develop your grip, timing and stick bounce, you have already been playing this rudiment in fills. Therefore the better you play this rudiment on its own as an exercise, the better your fills will sound!

Double stroke roll - Two hits with each hand.

This is the second most important rudiment to master. Practice slowly to start to get used to the sticking. Aim to get the double stroke roll to be as even as the single stroke roll.

To play a good single stroke or double stroke roll let the sticks bounce to create a fluid motion, make sure all notes are evenly placed and keep all hits the same volume.

Signing off and moving on
• *Play both rudiments for one minute each with a click track* •
Gold - 120bpm
Silver - 90bpm
Bronze - 60bpm

Paradiddle - Mixing single and double hits.

This rudiment mixes single and double strokes together, so will require a bit of practice to master. The paradiddle gets its name from the way it sounds when played. ('Pa' and 'Ra' are the two single strokes and 'Diddle' is the double stroke). Saying 'pa-ra-di-ddle' as you play may help. Make sure that this rudiment sounds as even as the single and double stroke rolls.

Using your rudiments

Having played these rudiments on just one drum or practice pad, it is important to play them on the drum kit so that we understand why we are spending our precious time practicing them. Here are a few ideas of how to apply rudiments to fills:

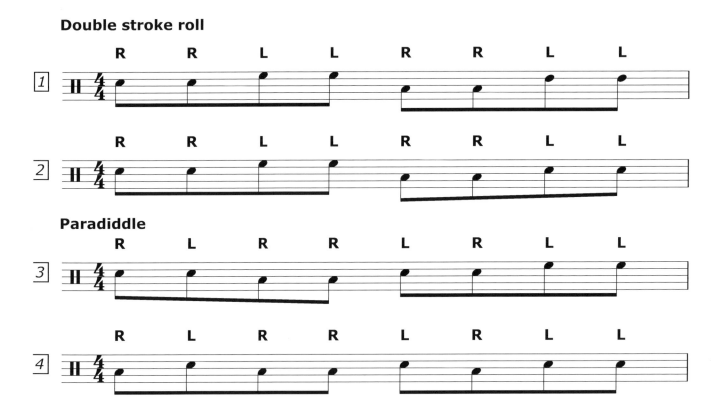

If you feel comfortable with these fills, try making more fills using double stroke rolls and paradiddles.

Signing off and moving on
• *Play paradiddles for one minute with a click track* •
Gold - 120bpm
Silver - 90bpm
Bronze - 60bpm

Mind the gap

o
Whole Note

Half Note

Rest

We have now played grooves and fills with music, learnt about good technique and practiced some rudiments, so it's now time to learn a little bit of the theory we need to understand to continue our development and create some space in our playing.

Checklist

By the end of this chapter you should be able to achieve the following:

- **Understand what a note value is**

- **Identify whole notes, half notes and quarter notes and state their respective values**

- **Identify whole note, half note and quarter note rests and state their respective values**

- **Play reading exercises containing whole notes, half notes, quarter notes and their respective rests**

- **Play fills that contain rests with various grooves in four bar phrases**

- **Create and play fills that contain rests**

- **Play shorter fills that last less than one bar**

As in previous chapters, use this page as an end of chapter test. When you have completed chapter four, come back to this page and see if you can complete the list above.

For information on
Backbone Drums Lesson Manager visit:
www.backbonedrums.com

Note values and rests

In this book we have talked about quarter notes and eighth notes, but where do they get there names from? As long as you understand some very basic maths the answer is very simple.

- **The name given to a note refers to its 'value'.**

- **The value of a note refers to how long it lasts until you play another note**

Here are the three biggest notes and their values:

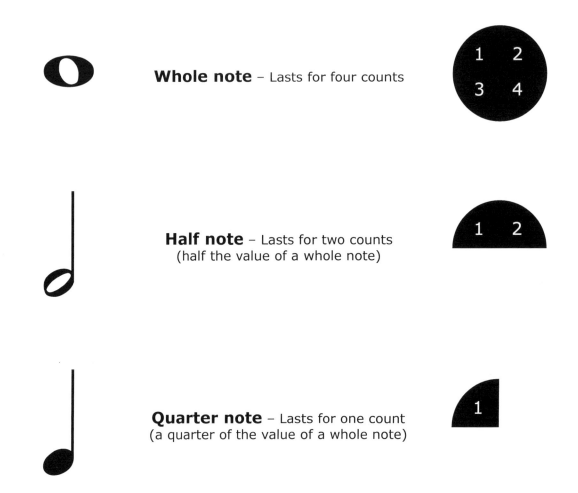

Whole note – Lasts for four counts

Half note – Lasts for two counts
(half the value of a whole note)

Quarter note – Lasts for one count
(a quarter of the value of a whole note)

When we talk about a note lasting for several counts, you have to imagine the note being held as if you were blowing a trumpet. With a trumpet, the longer you blow, the longer the note lasts. With a drum there is no way to make a note last any longer than one hit, so we are therefore not actually holding the note or making it last, but instead are just waiting for the correct amount of time until we play the next note.

Whole notes - 4 counts

Whole note   **Whole note rest**

The note written on the snare drum line in the first bar of the stave above is a 'whole note'.
To play a whole note, hit on count '1' and hold it (wait) for counts '2', '3' and '4'.

The block hanging from the second line down in the second bar is a 'whole note rest'.
If you see a whole note rest, DON'T play anything for 4 counts.

Half notes - 2 counts

Half notes   **Half note rests**

The notes written on the snare drum line in the first bar of the stave above are 'half notes'.
To play a half note, hit on whichever number it appears and hold it (wait) for the next count.
e.g. play on count '1' and hold it (wait) for count '2'.

The blocks sitting on the third line down in the second bar are 'half note rests'.
If you see a half note rest, DON'T play for 2 counts.

Quarter notes - 1 count

Quarter notes   **Quarter note rests**

The notes written on the snare drum line in the first bar of the stave above are 'quarter notes'.
To play a quarter note, only hit on the count that it appears.

The wavy lines in the second bar are 'quarter note rests'. If you see a quarter note rest, DON'T play for 1 count.

Mixing basic note values and rests

The following snare drum exercises mix whole notes, half notes, quarter notes and rests, and will get you used to leaving gaps in your playing.

Play each exercise separately and then play the whole page as one exercise.

<hr>

Signing off and moving on
• Play the entire page with a click track •
Gold - 120bpm
Silver - 90bpm
Bronze - 60bpm

Fills with rests

We have now looked at several different note values and rests, so here are some fills with rests in which create some gaps in our playing. Sometimes leaving a space can sound better than filling every gap with lots of notes.

Remember these fills are written out as a cymbal line and a drum line. If you find them confusing to work out, work out the drum part and cymbal part separately and then combine them.

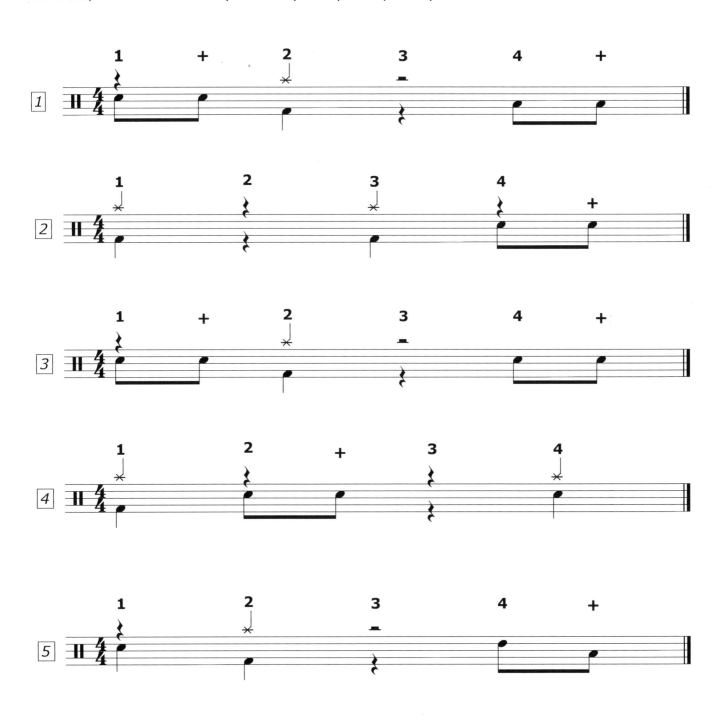

Copyright © D. Hazlewood

Create your own fills with rests

Using all notes and rests covered so far, create some fills of your own. There is no need to be too complicated, but instead focus on your timing.

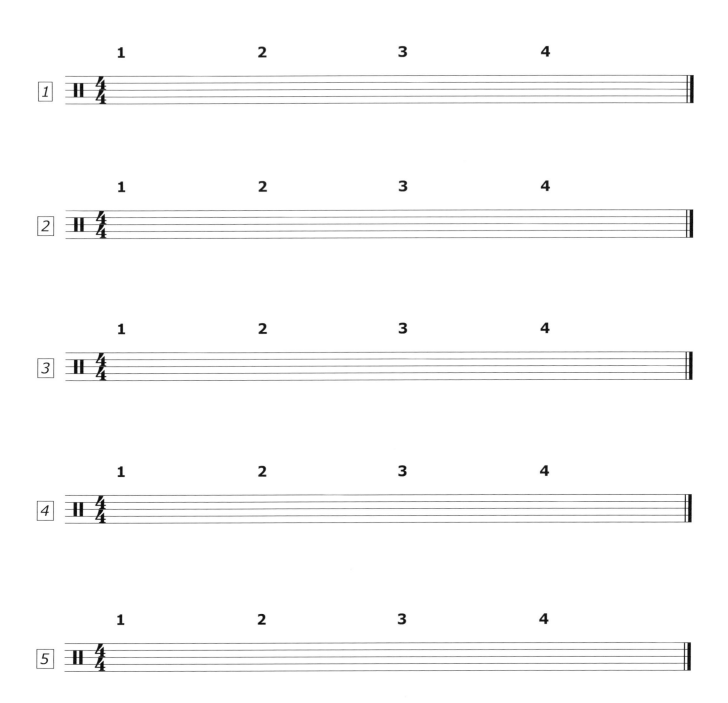

Signing off and moving on
• Play each fill in four bar phrases with a rock or pop backing track •
Gold - 110bpm
Silver - 85bpm
Bronze - 75bpm

Part bar fills

So far all of the fills we have looked at have taken up a whole bar, it is worth noting that a fill doesn't have to last a whole bar and sometimes works better when it is shorter. If you want a shorter fill in the fourth bar of a phrase, you just need to play the groove for a bit longer before you start the fill.

There are 4 counts in a bar, so if you want a fill that is only 2 counts long, you will need to play 2 more counts of groove before starting the fill. (Two counts groove plus two counts fill = four counts). If you want a fill that is three counts long, you will need to play 1 more count of groove before starting the fill (one count groove plus three counts fill = four counts).

Have a look at the following examples and then play each of them as your fourth bar within a four bar phrase.

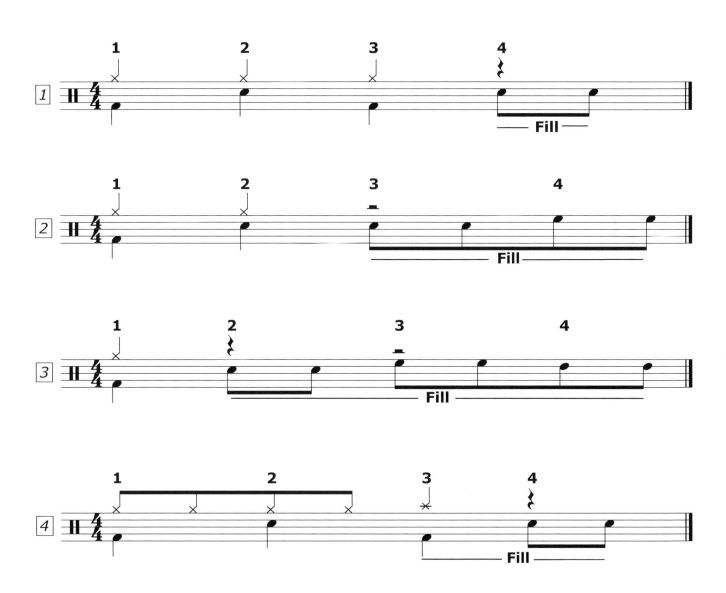

Create your own part bar fills

Using the templates below fill the gaps to create some of your own part bar fills. You can use eighth notes, quarter notes, quarter note rests and half note rests.

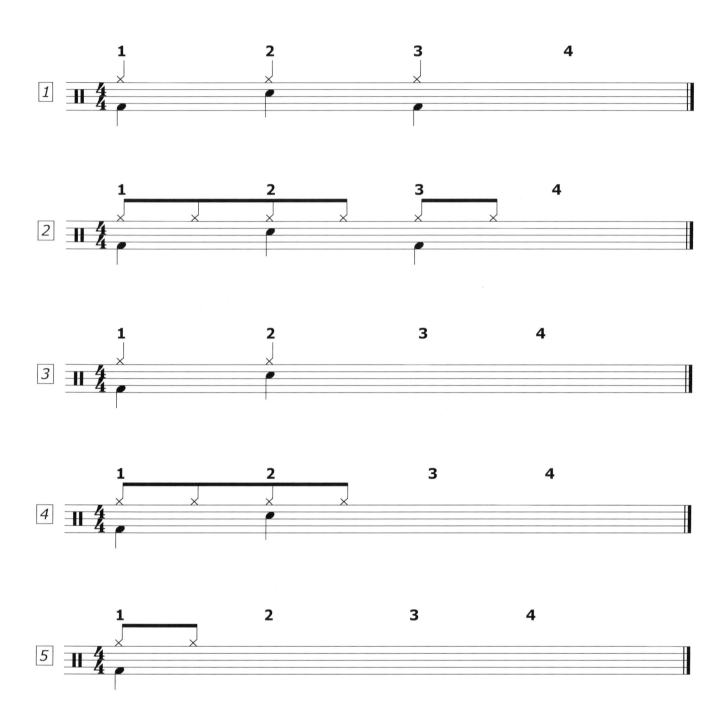

Copyright © D. Hazlewood

Make room for some more

A Sixteenth Note

Four Sixteenth Notes joined

In chapter three, we are going to look at some new notes called sixteenth notes. Just as the other notes we have looked at get their names from their relationship to a whole note so do sixteenth notes. There are sixteen sixteenth notes to a whole note. A single sixteenth note looks different to an eighth note because it has two tails instead of just one.

Checklist

By the end of this chapter, you should be able to achieve the following:

- **Play sixteenth note grooves**

- **Play sixteenth note fills**

- **Read music containing quarter notes, eighth notes and sixteenth notes**

- **Play fills mixing quarter notes, eighth notes and sixteenth notes**

- **Create your own fills mixing quarter notes, eighth notes and sixteenth notes**

- **Play some different bass drum patterns with sixteenth note hi-hats**

As in other chapters use this page as an end of chapter test. When you have completed chapter five, come back to this page and see if you can complete the list above.

For information on
Backbone Drums Lesson Manager visit:
www.backbonedrums.com

Sixteenth note groove

This next groove is similar to the quarter note and eighth note grooves in that the snare and bass pattern is the same, but the hi hat pattern has changed again. You are now going to play so many notes that to play at a reasonable speed, you will be using both hands on the hi-hats.

Your lead (stronger) hand still plays the '1 + 2 + 3 + 4 +' that it did in the eighth note groove, but your other hand will play in between each note filling the gaps and changing the count to '1 e + a 2 e + a 3 e + a 4 e + a'.

This also means that your lead hand will have to play the snare drum as well as the hi-hat.

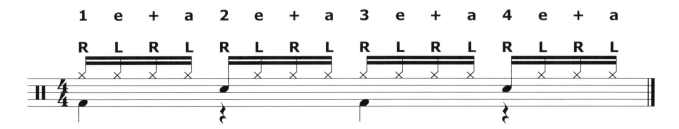

When you are comfortable with this groove, start to loop (repeat) it and see how many times you can play through with no mistakes. When you can play at least ten times through have a go at playing it along with a backing track.

Sixteenth note fill

As well as using sixteenth notes in grooves, we can play them in fills. Below is a basic fill using sixteenth notes.

Try playing the groove and then the fill at the same speed without speeding up or slowing down. When you are comfortable have a go at alternating between the groove and fill.

Signing off and moving on
• *Loop just the groove consistently with a rock or pop backing track* •
Gold - 110bpm
Silver - 85bpm
Bronze - 75bpm

Sixteenth note four bar phrase

Here is the groove and fill together in a four bar phrase. Watch out for the crash at the start of each four bar phrase.

One handed sixteenth note groove

To be able to play this groove on the ride, you will have to play the cymbal pattern with just one hand. This makes your lead hand work a lot harder and will therefore have to be played much slower. Try the four bar phrase below playing the groove on the ride with just your lead hand and then changing to play the fill with two hands.

Signing off and moving on
• *Play the first four bar phrase looped with a rock or pop backing track* •
Gold - 110bpm
Silver - 75bpm
Bronze - 60bpm

Mixing quarter notes, eighth notes and sixteenth notes

We can now add our new notes to the other notes we have looked at so far. Play the following exercises with a click track, one at a time to start and then play the whole page.

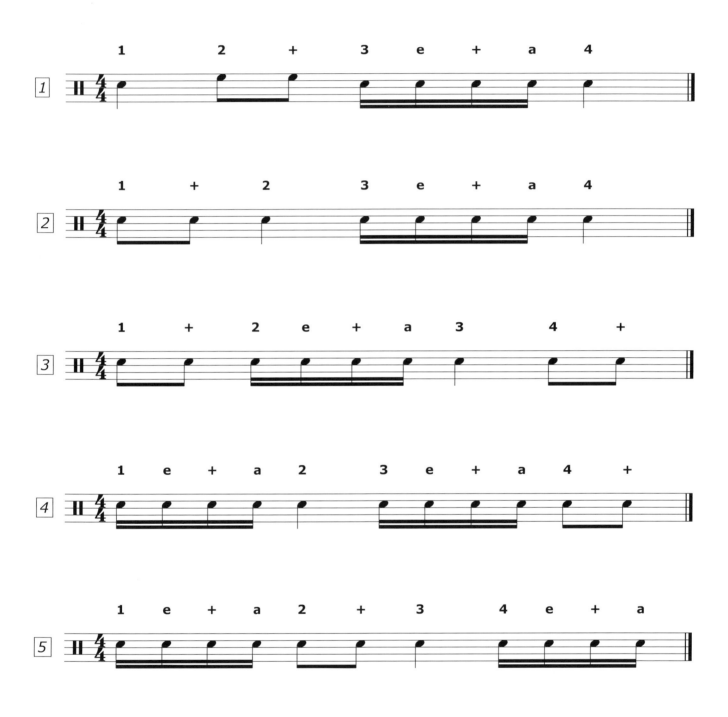

Quarter notes, eighth notes and sixteenth notes around the drums as fills

Now you are comfortable with the timing of playing quarter notes, eighth notes and sixteenth notes, we can start to play the same rhythms around the drums in our fills.

Try the following fills on their own, and then play in four bar phrases. First play with the quarter note groove and then when you are comfortable with that use the eight note groove and then the sixteenth note groove.

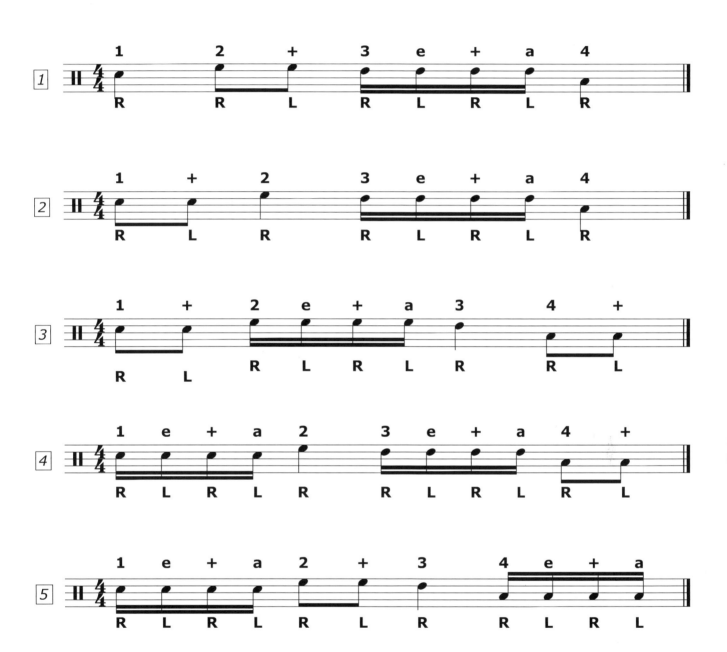

Copyright © D. Hazlewood

Create your own fills using quarter notes, eighth notes and sixteenth notes

Use the blank manuscript below to make your own fills. Feel free to use any of the notes and rests that you have covered so far, be as creative as you like, but be careful of your timing.

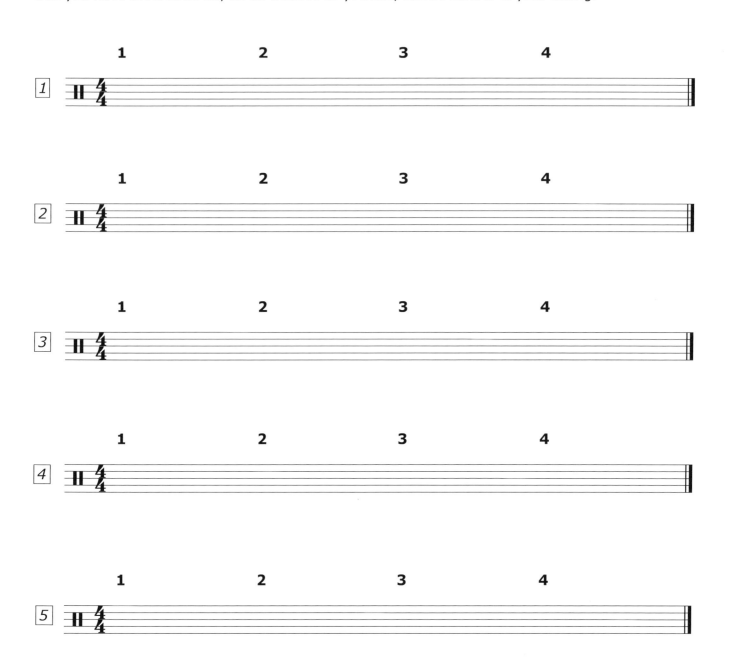

Signing off and moving on
• *Play any of your own fills with any groove in four bar phrases with a rock or pop backing track* •
Gold - 110bpm
Silver - 85bpm
Bronze - 60bpm

Sixteenth note grooves with varied bass patterns

Here are some more sixteenth note grooves played with some of the same snare and bass patterns from earlier in the book.

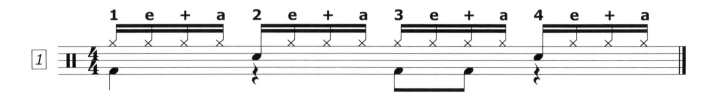

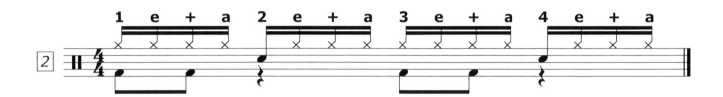

When you are comfortable with these grooves, have a go at the same patterns but with just one hand playing the cymbal part on the ride.

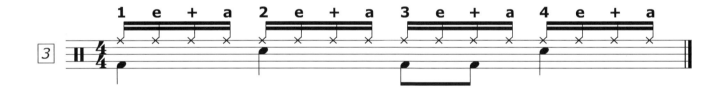

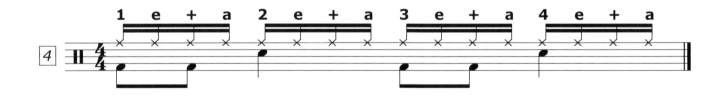

Signing off and moving on
• *Play grooves 1 and 2 only looped with a rock or pop backing track* •
Gold - 110bpm
Silver - 85bpm
Bronze - 60bpm

Three's a crowd

Eighth Notes Triplets

In chapter six, we are going to look at some grooves and fills that are a bit different to anything else we have looked at so far. We are going to look at some 'triplet' notes, which are notes in groups of three.

Checklist

By the end of this chapter you should be able to achieve the following:

- **Play eighth note triplet grooves**

- **Play eighth note triplet fills**

- **Play along with triplet feel backing tracks**

- **Read music containing quarter notes and eighth note triplets**

- **Play fills mixing quarter notes and eighth note triplets**

- **Create your own fills mixing quarter notes and eighth note triplets**

As in previous chapters, use this page as an end of chapter test. When you have completed chapter six, come back to this page and see if you can complete the list above.

For information on
Backbone Drums Lesson Manager visit:
www.backbonedrums.com

Eighth note triplet groove

All note values covered so far have had a very straight and even feel to them. Eighth notes are written in groups of two or four, and sixteenth notes are written in groups of four. These notes works well in a lot of musical situations, but not all. A lot of music has a 'swing' or 'shuffle' feel to it and requires different notes to work. This is where triplets come in. Triplet notes are grouped into three and give music a 'swing'.

Every note value has an equivalent 'triplet' brother, which means that for every two 'non triplet' notes, there will be three notes in its triplet version.

When counted out loud this will sound like '1 iron, 2 iron, 3 iron, 4 iron.

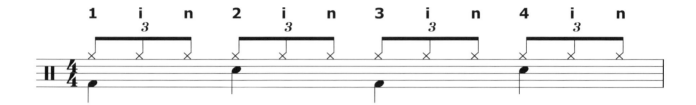

Practice this groove with backing tracks and really focus on making sure that your notes are nice and even. A row of eighth note triplets should be as even as a row of eighth notes or sixteenth notes, they are just at a different speed. Make sure you are not getting any awkward rhythms or pauses when you are playing.

Eighth note triplet fill

Eighth note triplets also work well in fills, but the sticking may initially feel slightly strange as your lead hand swaps on every count.

Loop the bar below with your bass drum playing every quarter note to develop nice even eighth note triplets and get used to your lead hand swapping.

Signing off and moving on
• *Loop just the groove consistently with a blues backing track* •
Gold - 85bpm
Silver - 70bpm
Bronze - 60bpm

Now play the eighth note triplets around the drums as a fill.
Note that the last group of three is played back on the first tom to avoid crossing your arms.

Four bar phrase

When you are happy playing the groove and fill at a constant speed, play the groove and the fill in four bar phrases. The groove is written to be played on the hi-hats but will sound nice on the ride as well so play it both ways.

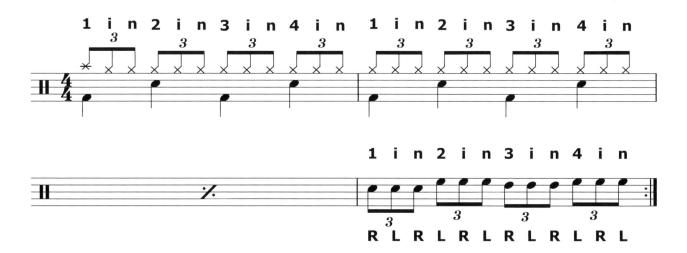

Mixing quarter notes and eighth note triplets

You can play eighth note triplets with any other notes, but this can create some timing issues, so for now we are only going to mix them with quarter notes. Play the following exercises one at a time and then play the whole page. Make sure you have a strong count and keep the numbers even with the in-between counts well spaced.

Sticking - Below each exercise is a suggested sticking pattern, which will help make your rhythms flow and will hopefully make the page easier to play as a whole piece.

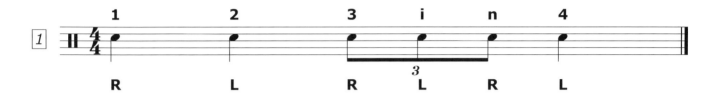

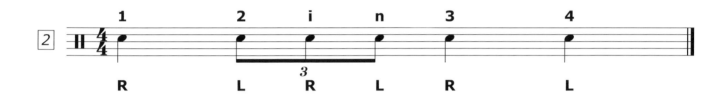

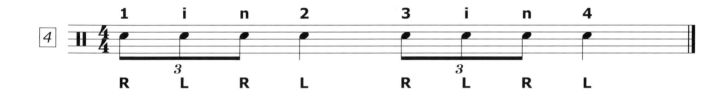

Signing off and moving on
• Play the entire page with a click track •
Gold - 120bpm
Silver - 90bpm
Bronze - 60bpm

Quarter notes and eighth notes triplets around the drums as fills

Taking the rhythms from the previous page, we can start to play them around the drums in fills.

Try the following fills on their own to start with, and then play in four bar phrases. Play with the eighth note triplet groove and also the very first quarter note groove from chapter 1.

Sticking - Be careful now and pay attention to which hand is leading and which drums you are playing.

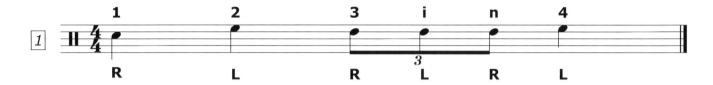

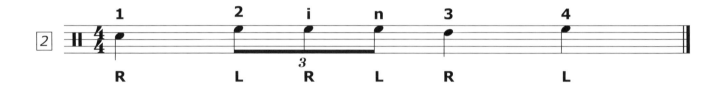

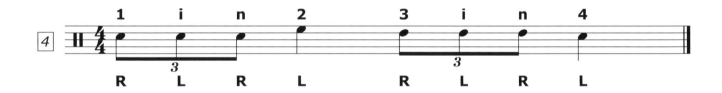

Signing off and moving on
• *Play each of these fills with either quarter note or eighth note triplet grooves in four bar phrases with blues backing tracks* •
Gold - 120bpm
Silver - 90bpm
Bronze - 60bpm

Create your own fills using quarter notes and eighth note triplets

Use the blank manuscript below to make your own fills using quarter notes and eighth note triplets.

Sticking - Be careful when writing and playing your fills that you don't cross your arms over. If it helps write the sticking underneath each line.

```
            1              2              3              4
1   ‖ 4/4 ═══════════════════════════════════════════════════ ‖

            1              2              3              4
2   ‖ 4/4 ═══════════════════════════════════════════════════ ‖

            1              2              3              4
3   ‖ 4/4 ═══════════════════════════════════════════════════ ‖

            1              2              3              4
4   ‖ 4/4 ═══════════════════════════════════════════════════ ‖
```

Signing off and moving on
• Play any of your own fills with any groove in four bar phrases with a blues backing track •
Gold - 85bpm
Silver - 75bpm
Bronze - 60bpm

Triplet rudiments

Previously we looked at rudiments using eighth notes, so here are two rudiments using eighth note triplets.

All of the points mentioned in chapter three will need to be applied here, so maybe read over that chapter again to refresh your memory before attempting these rudiments.

Triple stroke roll

Triplet rudiment

Triplet rudiments in fills

Here are two ideas of how these rudiments can be played in fills. Play each of them in four bar phrases.

Signing off and moving on
• *Play triple stroke roll and triplet rudiment for one minute with a click track* •
Gold - 120bpm
Silver - 90bpm
Bronze - 60bpm

The end of
the beginning

That's it... having now worked through this book you should have a good basic understanding of your role as a drummer, how the drum kit works as a musical instrument and time keeping tool, and how music is written.

Checklist

You should now be able to achieve the following:

- **Understand the role of a drummer**
- **Read, play and write basic grooves and fills**
- **Understand and read note values and rests**
- **Play in time with music**
- **Demonstrate good technique and posture**
- **Play clean and even rudiments**

This is the final chapter and brings together everything you have learnt so far. If you struggle on any aspect within these last few pages, you may need to refer back to previous chapters to refresh your memory.

Have fun and good luck!

For information on
Backbone Drums Lesson Manager visit:
www.backbonedrums.com

Drum charts

A chart is an entire song or piece of music written out in notation and is like a map for a song telling you what to play for each section.

A drum chart can be for snare drum or full drum kit, and may well contain repeat markings and other information.

Charting success

Over the next few pages there are several charts, which need to be played with either a click track or backing track. Take your time to look over these charts and work through each one slowly before attempting to play with backing tracks or click tracks.

When playing these charts use your ears, don't concentrate so much on reading that your timing suffers. Remember a drummer's job is to keep time, it is better to make a few mistakes but keep perfect time than to get every note correct but play out of time!

Backing tracks for full drum kit are provided in two formats:

1. Backing track with drum track

2. Backing track with click

To sign off each chart you should play along with the backing track with click track.

Snare drum pieces should be played with the click tracks provided (tracks 22 – 34 on your CD). Start slowly and gradually increase the tempo as you gain confidence.

Chart 1 - Basic note values

This first chart is for snare drum and contains basic notes and rests as well, as a short repeat section.

Count in:

1 - 2 - 1 2 3 4

Signing off and moving on

• *Play the entire chart with a click track* •
Gold - 110bpm
Silver - 90bpm
Bronze - 70bpm

Chart 2 - Quarter note rock - 100bpm

This chart is for the whole drum kit and is a rock tune based around a quarter note groove. The piece is 16 bars long and is broken into four sections. Each section is four bars long.

Backing track numbers for this chart are:

14 - With drums

15 - With click

Count in:
1 - 2 - 1 2 3 4

Copyright © D. Hazlewood

Chart 3 - Eighth note pop - 80bpm

This is another chart for the whole drum kit and is a pop tune based around an eighth note groove. The piece is sixteen bars long and is broken into four sections, each four bars long.

Backing tracks for this chart are:

16 - With drums

17 - With click

Count in:

1 - 2 - 1 2 3 4

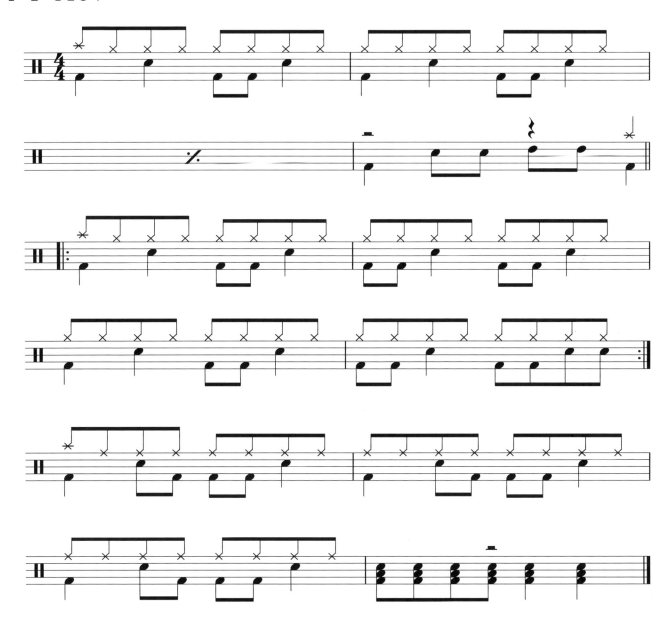

> ### Signing off and moving on
> • *Play the entire chart with backing track 17* •
> **Gold - Good timing and no mistakes**
> **Silver - Good timing with 3 or fewer mistakes**
> **Bronze - Acceptable timing with 3 or fewer mistakes**

Chart 4 - Basic rhythms

This chart is a just for the snare drum and is an exercise in reading basic rhythms and rests.

Count in:

1 - 2 - 1 2 3 4

Copyright © D. Hazlewood

Chart 5 - Sixteenth note rock - 75bpm

This chart is for the whole drum kit and is a rock tune based around a sixteenth note groove.

Backing track numbers for this chart are:

18 - With drums

19 - With click

Count in:
1 - 2 - 1 2 3 4

Signing off and moving on
• *Play the entire chart with backing track 19* •
Gold - Good timing and no mistakes
Silver - Good timing with 3 or fewer mistakes
Bronze - Acceptable timing with 3 or fewer mistakes

Chart 6 - Reading eighth note triplets

This chart is a just for the snare drum and is an exercise in reading eighth note triplets with whole notes, half notes and quarter notes with their respective rests.

Count in:
1 - 2 - 1 2 3 4

Copyright © D. Hazlewood

Chart 7 - Triplet blues - 65bpm

This chart is for a blues tune and is based around an eighth note triplet groove. It has a slightly different format to the previous tunes as it is in a 'twelve bar blues' arrangement. In a twelve bar blues piece the music follows a particular chord progression that gives it a very specific sound and is just like a twelve bar phrase. This tune is to be played through twice, once using hi hats and once using the ride cymbal.

Backing tracks for this chart are:

20 - With drums

21 - With click

Count in:
1 - 2 - 1 2 3 4

Signing off and moving on
• *Play the entire chart with backing track 21* •
Gold - Good timing and no mistakes
Silver - Good timing with 3 or fewer mistakes
Bronze - Acceptable timing with 3 or fewer mistakes

Chart markings test

Fill in the blanks below and then check your answers over the page.

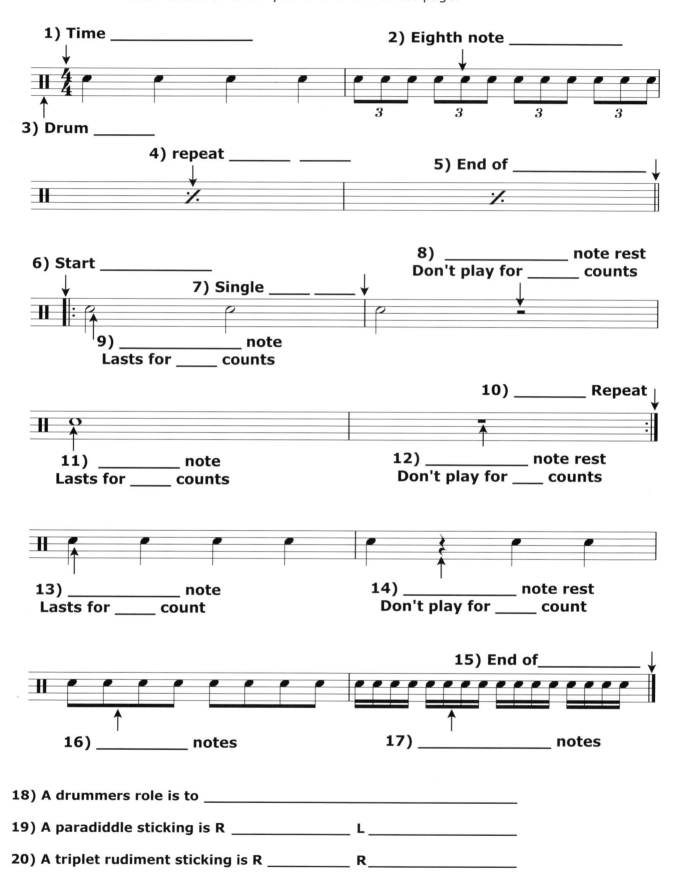

1) Time _____

2) Eighth note _____

3) Drum _____

4) repeat _____ _____

5) End of _____

6) Start _____

7) Single _____ _____

8) _____ **note rest**
Don't play for _____ **counts**

9) _____ **note**
Lasts for _____ **counts**

10) _____ **Repeat**

11) _____ **note**
Lasts for _____ **counts**

12) _____ **note rest**
Don't play for ____ **counts**

13) _____ **note**
Lasts for _____ **count**

14) _____ **note rest**
Don't play for _____ **count**

15) End of_____

16) _____ **notes**

17) _____ **notes**

18) A drummers role is to _____

19) A paradiddle sticking is R _____ **L** _____

20) A triplet rudiment sticking is R _____ **R**_____

Answers over page

End of book test - Answers

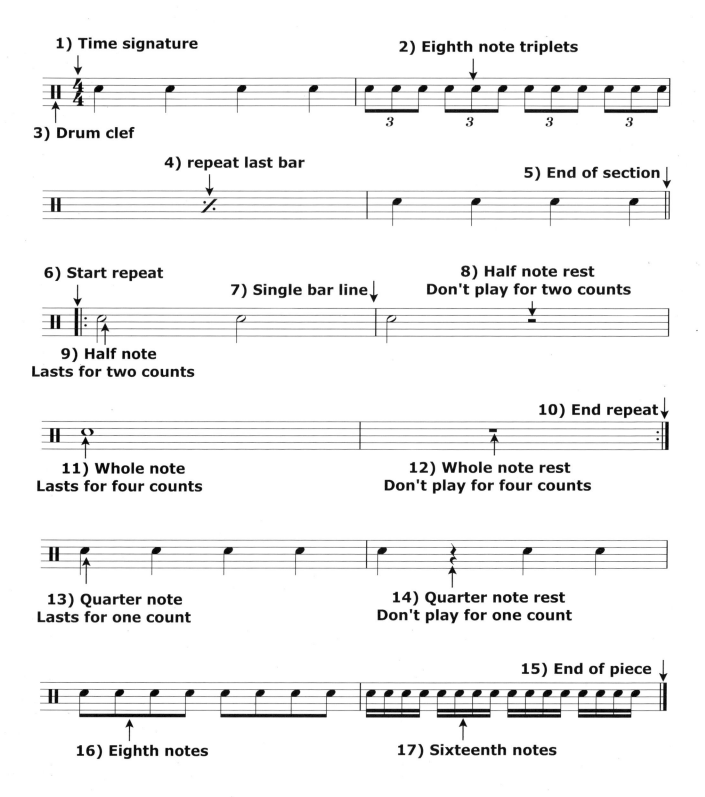

18) A drummers role is to keep time for a band

19) A paradiddle sticking is R L R R L R L L

20) A triplet rudiment sticking is R L L or L R R